SONGS OF GOD'S PEOPLE

The Church of Scotland
Supplement to the Church Hymnary
Third Edition

WORDS EDITION

Published on behalf of
The Panel on Worship
The Church of Scotland

OXFORD UNIVERSITY PRESS
1988

Oxford University Press, Walton Street, Oxford OX2 6DP

Oxford New York Toronto Melbourne Auckland
Delhi Bombay Calcutta Madras Karachi
Petaling Jaya Singapore Hong Kong Tokyo
Nairobi Dar es Salaam Cape Town

Associated companies in Berlin & Ibadan

Oxford is a trade mark of Oxford University Press

ISBN 0 19 197801 9

Acknowledgements for copyright words,
and an Index of Songs will be found
at the back of this book.

A Music Edition is also available

Printed in Scotland

FOREWORD

The Panel on Worship has been happy to respond to the request of the 1986 General Assembly 'to make available a selection of the best recent hymns in a supplement published for that purpose'.

One of the exciting features of recent years has been the considerable production of new words and music for worship, and in making a selection we have sought to represent the wide range of this material. The Panel is grateful to The Reverend John Bell who both convened the supplement committee and acted as its music editor.

These are *Songs of God's People*: songs which are being sung and which people have asked to sing, most of which have been recently written, but some of which are old favourites. We hope that they will serve to enrich the praise of God's people in ways that are contemporary and lively.

These songs reflect some of the varied strands of spirituality and renewal in the Church today. It is our earnest prayer that they will be used to encourage freshness and renewal in the worship of the whole Church.

ANDREW J. SCOBIE
Convener, Panel on Worship

PREFACE

This book is a tribute to the diversity of the Church, not just in its history and traditions but also in the preferences of people within a single denomination. God has made us all different and therefore it should be no surprise that people vary in their musical tastes as they vary in their dress sense. What is anathema to some—be it Gregorian Chant or Redemption Hymns— has been a means of grace to others. And so, in compiling and preparing this book, the committee endeavoured on the one hand not to be partisan, yet on the other not to include that which was so well known that its inclusion would have wasted space.

Here you will find songs, the vast majority of which have found a place and purpose in different parts of the Church and which represent a variety of 'seams' of musical tradition. They range from Victorian favourites, which still hold value for many, to contemporary hymns from the English-speaking schools of writers, and to the simple responses of the Taizé Community in France.

Here, too, you will find songs of God's people in other countries. Having exported spiritual songs all over the world in the last two centuries, we must, as members of the One Holy Catholic Church, expect to receive the creative gifts which the Holy Spirit has encouraged elsewhere. But here also you will find songs in native British folk traditions, using tunes which both transcend age barriers and enable the Gospel to become rooted in our cultures.

Songs of God's People is intended to supplement existing hymnals. It is not envisaged as a book for choirs or musical specialists, but is for the people of God whether they worship in resplendent churches or draughty halls. Thus while there are some items which require a fair degree of musical skill for their best presentation, the bulk of these songs may be used immediately by the most reluctant of organists or pianists and by the most timid of congregations.

To increase the practicality and appeal of this book, guitar chords have been included for many items and well-known tunes are offered as alternatives to new melodies. Many items are designed to be sung unaccompanied and in unison, a reformed church tradition perhaps over-neglected since organs became established in our sanctuaries.

It is the hope and prayer of those responsible for this publication that it will enrich the worship life of our congregations, extend the range of our choices in hymnody, and deepen our love and praise of God.

The Church of Scotland owes its gratitude to those members who, rather than lamenting the dearth of new music, wrote to the committee suggesting most of the items included here; to members of the committee for their patience and sensitivity in what has not been the easiest of tasks; and to the staff of Oxford University Press and The Reverend Charles Robertson (Secretary of the Panel on Worship and of this committee) who have shown great reserves of tolerance and kindness in the various stages of the book's production. To all of these, I would add my personal appreciation for the privilege of being associated with this publication.

JOHN L. BELL
Convener, Supplement Committee

1

1 A holy baby is born in Judah's Bethlehem.
    He is Jesu, the son of Mary,
    He is Jesu, the son of God.

2 The simple shepherds soon left their sheep to search for him.

3 The magi three came to offer gifts and worship him.

4 To Egypt land his parents flew from Herod's wrath.

5 He grew in wisdom in Nazareth of Galilee.

6 He taught the teachers in the temple of Jerusalem.

7 In Jordan river the Holy Spirit came to him.

8 He brought the Kingdom of heaven to all believers.

9 Our sins and failings have nailed him to the cross to die.

10 God raised him up and brought him back to life again.

11 He is our Saviour and gives us all his peace and power.

12 Our Saviour's Spirit will be with us evermore.

T. Colvin

2

A new commandment that I give to you,
is to love one another as I have loved you;
is to love one another as I have loved you.
By this shall all know you are my disciples:
if you have love one for another;
by this shall all know you are my disciples:
if you have love one for another.

John 13: 34—35

3

Abba Father, let me be yours, and yours alone.
May my will for ever be evermore your own.
Never let my heart grow cold, never let me go,
Abba Father, let me be yours, and yours alone.

D. Bilbrough

4

1 All over the world the Spirit is moving,
   all over the world as the prophet said it would be;
   all over the world there's a mighty revelation
   of the glory of the Lord, as the waters cover the sea.

2 Deep down in my heart the Spirit is moving,
   deep down in my heart as the prophet said it would be;
   deep down in my heart there's a mighty revelation
   of the glory of the Lord, as the waters cover the sea.

Anon.

5

Alleluia, alleluia!

6

Alleluia, alleluia!

7

Alleluia, alleluia, give thanks to the risen Lord!
Alleluia, alleluia, give praise to his name.

1 Jesus is Lord of all the earth.
   He is the King of creation.

2 Spread the good news through all the earth,
   Jesus has died and has risen:

3 We have been crucified with Christ —
   now we shall live for ever:

4 God has proclaimed the just reward —
   life for the world, alleluia!

5 Come, let us praise the living God,
   joyfully sing to our Saviour!

D. Fishel

8

Hallelujah, my Father, for giving us your Son;
sending him into the world to be given up for men,
knowing we would bruise him and smite him from the earth:
hallelujah, my Father, in his death is my birth,
hallelujah, my Father, in his life is my life.

T. Cullen

9

1 Amazing grace! (how sweet the sound!)
that saved a wretch like me!
I once was lost, but now am found,
was blind, but now I see.

2 'Twas grace that taught my heart to fear,
and grace my fears relieved;
How precious did that grace appear
the hour I first believed!

3 Through many dangers, toils and snares,
I have already come;
'Tis grace has brought me safe thus far,
and grace will lead me home.

4 The Lord has promised good to me,
his word my hope secures;
he will my shield and portion be
as long as life endures.

J. Newton

10

1 As man and woman we were made,
that love be found and life begun;
so praise the Lord who made us two,
and praise the Lord when two are one:
praise for the love that comes to life
through child or parent, husband, wife.

2 Now Jesus lived and gave his love
to make our life and loving new;
so celebrate with him today,
and drink the joy he offers you
that makes the simple moment shine
and changes water into wine.

3 And Jesus died to live again,
so praise the love that, come what may,
can bring the dawn and clear the skies,
and waits to wipe all tears away,
and let us hope for what shall be,
believing where we cannot see.

4 Then spread the table, clear the hall,
and celebrate till day is done;
let peace go deep between us all,
and joy be shared by everyone:
laugh and make merry with your friends,
and praise the love that never ends!

B. Wren

11

1 Before the world began
one Word was there;
grounded in God he was,
rooted in care;
by him all things were made,
in him was love displayed,
through him God spoke and said,
I am for you.

2 Life found in him its source,
death found its end;
light found in him its course,
darkness its friend;
for neither death nor doubt
nor darkness can put out
the glow of God, the shout:
I am for you.

3 The Word was in the world
which from him came;
unrecognised he was,
unknown by name;
one with all humankind,
with the unloved aligned,
convincing sight and mind:
I am for you.

4 All who received the Word
by God were blessed;
sisters and brothers they
of earth's fond guest.
So did the Word of Grace
proclaim in time and space
and with a human face,
I am for you.

J. Bell and G. Maule based on John 1: 1—13

12

Behold the lamb of God,
behold the lamb of God;
he takes away the sin,
the sin of the world.

John 1: 29

13

Bind us together, Lord,
bind us together
with cords that cannot be broken.
Bind us together, Lord,
bind us together,
O bind us together with love.

1 There is only one God.
There is only one King.
There is only one body;
that is why we sing.

2 Made for the glory of God,
purchased by his precious Son.
Born with the right to be clean,
for Jesus the victory has won.

3 You are the family of God.
You are the promise divine.
You are God's chosen desire.
You are the glorious new wine.

B. Gillman

14

1 Blessed assurance, Jesus is mine!
O what a foretaste of glory divine!
Heir of salvation, purchase of God;
born of his Spirit, washed in his blood.
This is my story, this is my song,
praising my Saviour all the day long.

2 Perfect submission, perfect delight,
visions of rapture burst on my sight;
angels descending, bring from above
echoes of mercy, whispers of love.

3 Perfect submission, all is at rest,
I in my Saviour am happy and blest;
watching and waiting, looking above,
filled with his goodness, lost in his love.

F. van Alstyne

15

Bless the Lord, my soul,
and bless his holy name.
Bless the Lord, my soul,
he rescues me from death.

Taizé Community

16

Blessing and honour, wisdom and wealth,
freedom to save or to sever:
these we proclaim belong to our God,
Lord of creation for ever.

1 Safe as the atom, unsplit in its shell,
strong as the sea in intention,
fine as the weave of the dragonfly's wing,
power is God's perfect invention.

2 Born of a woman and skilled at the lathe,
forfeiting glamour and glory,
God, in the flesh of a carpenter's son,
practised the power of a story.

3 Tempted to transform the stones into bread,
taunted to call help from heaven,
Christ showed how strength lay in carrying the cross,
forgiving seventy times seven.

4 Power is made perfect where weakness is strong;
weakness is meant for our healing;
healing is found at the feet of the poor
where God, as servant, is kneeling.

5 Made in the image of one who, unarmed,
challenged the great and the greedy,
ours is the privilege to claim and express
justice for all who are needy.

J. Bell and G. Maule

17

1 By cool Siloam's shady rill
how sweet the lily grows!
How sweet the breath beneath the hill
of Sharon's dewy rose!

2 Lo! such a child whose early feet
  the paths of peace have trod,
  whose secret heart with influence sweet
  is upward drawn to God.

3 By cool Siloam's shady rill
  the lily must decay,
  the rose that blooms beneath the hill
  must shortly fade away.

4 And soon, too soon, the wintry hour
  of man's maturer age
  will shake the soul with sorrow's power
  and stormy passion's rage.

5 O thou whose infant feet were found
  within thy Father's shrine,
  whose years, with changeless virtue crowned,
  were all alike divine.

6 Dependent on thy bounteous breath
  we seek thy grace alone,
  in childhood, manhood, age, and death
  to keep us still thine own.

R. Heber

18

By the waters, the waters of Babylon
we lay down and wept,
and wept for you Zion:
we remember, we remember,
we remember you Zion.

Psalm 137: 1

19

1 Christ be beside me,
  Christ be before me,
  Christ be behind me,
  King of my heart.
  Christ be within me,
  Christ be below me,
  Christ be above me,
  never to part.

2 Christ on my right hand,
  Christ on my left hand,
  Christ all around me,
  shield in the strife.
  Christ in my sleeping,
  Christ in my sitting,
  Christ in my rising,
  light of my life.

3 Christ be in all hearts
thinking about me,
Christ be in all tongues
telling of me.
Christ be the vision
in eyes that see me,
in ears that hear me,
Christ ever be.

adapted from 'St Patrick's Breastplate'
(8th century) by J. Quinn, S.J.

20

1 Christ is alive! Let Christians sing.
His cross stands empty to the sky.
Let streets and homes with praises ring.
His love in death shall never die.

2 Christ is alive! No longer bound
to distant years in Palestine
he comes to claim the here and now
and dwell in every place and time.

3 Not throned afar, remotely high,
untouched, unmoved by human pains
but daily, in the midst of life,
our Saviour in the Godhead reigns.

4 In every insult, rift, and war
where colour, scorn or wealth divide,
he suffers still, yet loves the more,
and lives, though ever crucified.

5 Christ is alive, and comes to bring
good news to this and every age,
till earth and all creation ring
with joy, with justice, love and praise.

B. Wren

21

1 Christ's is the world in which we move;
Christ's are the folk we're summoned to love;
Christ's is the voice which calls us to care,
and Christ is the one who meets us here.

To the lost Christ shows his face,
to the unloved he gives his embrace,
to those who cry in pain or disgrace,
Christ makes, with his friends, a touching place.

2 Feel for the people we most avoid —
   strange or bereaved or never employed.
   Feel for the women and feel for the men
   who fear that their living is all in vain.

3 Feel for the parents who've lost their child,
   feel for the women whom men have defiled,
   feel for the baby for whom there's no breast,
   and feel for the weary who find no rest.

4 Feel for the lives by life confused,
   riddled with doubt, in loving abused;
   feel for the lonely heart, conscious of sin,
   which longs to be pure but fears to begin.

J. Bell and G. Maule

22

1 Colours of day dawn into the mind,
   the sun has come up, the night is behind.
   Go down to the city, into the street
   and let's give the message to the people we meet.
   So light up the fire and let the flame burn,
   open the door, let Jesus return.
   Take seeds of his Spirit, let the fruit grow,
   tell the people of Jesus, let his love show.

2 Go through the park, on into the town;
   the sun still shines on, it never goes down.
   The light of the world is risen again;
   the people of darkness are needing our friend.

3 Open your eyes, look into the sky,
   the darkness has come, the sun came to die.
   The evening draws on, the sun disappears,
   but Jesus is living, and his Spirit is near.

S. McClellan, J. Pac, and K. Ryecroft

23

1 Come with me, come wander, come welcome the world
where strangers might smile or where stones may be hurled;
come leave what you cling to, lay down what you clutch,
and find with hands empty that hearts can hold much.
   Sing hey for the carpenter leaving his tools!
   Sing hey for the Pharisees leaving their rules!
   Sing hey for the fishermen leaving their nets!
   Sing hey for the people who leave their regrets!

2 Come walk in my company, come sleep by my side,
come savour a lifestyle with nothing to hide,
come sit at my table and eat with my friends,
discovering that love which the world never ends.

3 Come share in my laughter, come close to my fears,
come find yourself washed with the kiss of my tears,
come stand close at hand while I suffer and die,
and find in three days how I never will lie.

4 Come leave your possessions, come share out your treasure,
come give and receive without method or measure,
come loose every bond that's resisting the Spirit,
enabling the earth to be yours to inherit.

J. Bell and G. Maule

24

Do not be afraid, for I have redeemed you.
I have called you by your name; you are mine.

1 When you walk through the waters I'll be with you,
   you will never sink beneath the waves.

2 When the fire is burning all around you,
   you will never be consumed by the flames.

3 When the fear of loneliness is looming,
   then remember I am at your side.

4 When you dwell in the exile of the stranger,
   remember you are precious in my eyes.

5 You are mine, O my child; I am your Father,
   and I love you with a perfect love.

G. Markland
from Isaiah 43: 1—4

25

Dona nobis pacem in terra;
dona nobis pacem, Domine.

(Grant us peace on earth;
grant us peace, O Lord.)

26

1 Father, we adore you,
lay our lives before you:
how we love you!

2 Jesus, we adore you,
lay our lives before you:
how we love you!

3 Spirit, we adore you,
lay our lives before you:
how we love you!

T. Coelho

27

1 Father, we love you, we worship and adore you,
Glorify your name in all the earth,
glorify your name, glorify your name,
glorify your name in all the earth.

2 Jesus, we love you, we worship and adore you,

3 Spirit, we love you, we worship and adore you,

D. Adkins

28

1 For the bread that we have eaten,
for the wine that we have tasted,
for the life that you have given,
Father, Son, and Holy Spirit,
we will praise you.

2 For the life of Christ within us
turning all our fears to freedom,
helping us to live for others,

3 For the strength of Christ to lead us
in our living and our dying,
in the end, with all your people,

B. Wren

29

1 For the healing of the nations,
Lord, we pray with one accord;
for a just and equal sharing
of the things that earth affords.
To a life of love in action
help us rise and pledge our word.

2 Lead us, Father, into freedom;
from despair your world release,
that, redeemed from war and hatred,
all may come and go in peace.
Show us how through care and goodness
fear will die and hope increase.

3 All that kills abundant living,
let it from the earth be banned;
pride of status, race, or schooling,
dogmas that obscure your plan.
In our common quest for justice
may we hallow life's brief span.

4 You, Creator-God, have written
your great name on humankind;
for our growing in your likeness
bring the life of Christ to mind;
that by our response and service
earth its destiny may find.

F . Kaan

30

1 From creation's start, there has been a story
told from age to age, of the Maker's glory:
painted in the sky, sung in joy and sadness,
acted out in love, raged against in madness.

2 Though the love was there, men would not believe it;
blinded by their fears, they could not receive it.
Pride, oppression, hate, ride the world uncaring;
in the lust for life, we would die despairing.

3 Listen for the voice, it has never vanished,
though to death's dark night we had thought it banished;
hear it through the guns, from the prisons ringing,
from the long-denied, songs of freedom singing.

4 Hear it from the poor, crying for each other,
   from the sister scorned, reaching to a brother,
   from the wounded heart, touching us in pity,
   hear it from the cross, raised outside the city.

5 Everyone who hears with the heart and spirit
   knows the story true, life we shall inherit;
   what we give away shall return completed,
   so the song goes on, evermore repeated.

6 Glory be to God, mystery in giving,
   glory be to Jesus, one with us in living,
   glory to the Spirit, hurt among us mending,
   trinity of life, in the life unending.
   Glory be to God.

K. Galloway

31

Gabi Gabi
Bash' abazalwan', *(repeat)*
Siyoshiywa khona
Sidal' ubuzalwan'. *(repeat)*

Praise the Father,
liberator, Lord. (repeat)
He frees all the captives
and gives the hungry bread. (repeat)

South African traditional song
(no direct translation)

32

1 Gifts of bread and wine, gifts we've offered,
   fruits of labour, fruits of love:
   taken, offered, sanctified,
   blessed and broken; words of one who died:
       'Take my body, take my saving blood.'
       Gifts of bread and wine: Christ our Lord.

2 Christ our Saviour, living presence here,
   as he promised while on earth:
   'I am with you for all time,
   I am with you in this bread and wine.'

3 Through the Father, with the Spirit,
   one in union with the Son,
   for God's people, joined in prayer,
   faith is strengthened by the food we share.

C. McCann

33

1 God forgave my sin in Jesus' name —
  I've been born again in Jesus' name,
  and in Jesus' name I come to you
  to share his love as he told me to:
    He said,
    'Freely, freely you have received;
    freely, freely give!
    Go in my name and because you believe
    others will know that I live.'

2 All power is given in Jesus' name —
  in earth and heaven in Jesus' name,
  and in Jesus' name I come to you
  to share his power as he told me to:

                                      C. Owens

34

1 God's spirit is in my heart,
  he has called me and set me apart.
  This is what I have to do,
  what I have to do.
    He sent me to give the Good News to the poor,
    tell prisoners that they are prisoners no more,
    tell blind people that they can see,
    and set the downtrodden free,
    and go tell everyone the news that the Kingdom of God has come,
    and go tell everyone the news that God's Kingdom has come.

2 Just as the Father sent me,
  so I'm sending you out to be
  my witnesses throughout the world,
  the whole of the world.

3 Don't carry a load in your pack,
  you don't need two shirts on your back.
  A workman can earn his own keep,
  can earn his own keep.

4 Don't worry what you have to say,
  don't worry because on that day
  God's spirit will speak in your heart,
  will speak in your heart.

                                      A. Dale

35

1 God the Father of Creation,
source of life and energy,
your creative love so shapes us
that we share your liberty.
Teach us how to use this freedom
loving children all to be.

2 Jesus Christ our Lord and brother,
in your cross we see the way
to be servants for each other,
caring, suffering every day.
Teach us patience and obedience
never from your path to stray.

3 Holy Spirit, love that binds us
to the Father and the Son,
giver of the joy that fills us,
yours the peace that makes us one,
teach our hearts to be more open
so to pray 'God's will be done.'

4 Members of our Saviour's body,
here on earth his life to be,
though we stand as different people,
may we share the unity
of the Father, Son and Spirit,
perfect love in Trinity.

I. Cunningham

36

1 God who is everywhere present on earth,
no one can picture completely;
yet to the eye of the faithful he comes
and shows himself always uniquely.
Singing or sad, weeping or glad —
such are the glimpses of God that we're given.
Laughter and cheers, anger and tears —
these we inherit from earth and from heaven.

2 Shrouded in smoke or else high on the hill,
quaking with nature's own violence:
thus was the Lord found, frightening his folk,
but later he met them in silence.

3 God is the father who teaches his child
wisdom and values to cherish;
God is the mother who watches her young
and never will let her child perish.

4 Spear in the hand or with tears on the cheek;
Monarch and Shepherd and Lover:
many the faces that God calls his own
and many we've yet to discover.

5 Can we be certain of how the Lord looks,
deep though our faith and conviction,
when in the face of the Saviour we see
the smile of divine contradiction?

J. Bell and G. Maule

37

1 Great is thy faithfulness, O God my Father,
there is no shadow of turning with thee;
thou changest not, thy compassions they fail not,
as thou hast been thou for ever wilt be.
Great is thy faithfulness!
Great is thy faithfulness!
Morning by morning new mercies I see;
all I have needed thy hand hath provided —
great is thy faithfulness, Lord, unto me!

2 Summer and winter, and spring-time and harvest,
sun, moon and stars in their courses above,
join with all nature in manifold witness
to thy great faithfulness, mercy and love.

3 Pardon for sin and a peace that endureth,
thine own dear presence to cheer and to guide;
strength for today and bright hope for tomorrow,
blessings all mine, with ten thousand beside!

T. Chisholm

38

Hallelujah, hallelujah!

39

Halleluya! We sing your praises,
all our hearts are filled with gladness.
Halleluya! We sing your praises,
all our hearts are filled with gladness.

1 Christ the Lord to us said:
I am wine, I am bread,
I am wine, I am bread,
give to all who thirst and hunger.

2 Now he sends us all out
strong in faith, free of doubt,
strong in faith, free of doubt,
tell the world the joyful Gospel.

South African traditional song
(translated)

40

1 He is Lord, he is Lord;
   he is risen from the dead, and he is Lord;
   every knee shall bow, every tongue confess
   that Jesus Christ is Lord.

2 He is King, he is King;
   he will draw all nations to him, he is King;
   and the time shall be when the world shall sing
   that Jesus Christ is King.

3 He is love, he is love,
   he has shown us by his life that he is love;
   all his people sing with one voice of joy
   that Jesus Christ is love.

4 He is life, he is life;
   he has died to set us free and he is life;
   and he calls us all to live evermore,
   for Jesus Christ is life.

Anon.

41

1 Help us accept each other as Christ accepted us,
   teach us as sister, brother, each person to embrace.
   Be present, Lord, among us, and bring us to believe
   we are ourselves accepted and meant to love and live.

2 Let your acceptance change us, so that we may be moved
   in living situations to do the truth in love
   to practise your acceptance until we know by heart
   the meaning of forgiveness, and laughter's healing art.

3 Lord, for today's encounters with all who are in need,
   who hunger for acceptance, for righteousness and bread;
   we need new eyes for seeing, new hands for holding on:
   renew us with your Spirit, Lord, free us, make us one.

F. Kaan

42

1 Here hangs a man discarded,
   a scarecrow hoisted high,
   a nonsense pointing nowhere
   to all who hurry by.

2 Can such a clown of sorrows
   still bring a useful word
   where faith and love seem phantoms
   and every hope absurd?

3 Can he give help or comfort
   to lives by comfort bound
   when drums of dazzling progress
   give strangely hollow sound?

4 Life emptied of all meaning,
   drained out in bleak distress,
   can share in broken silence
   my deepest emptiness;

5 and love that freely entered
   the pit of life's despair
   can name our hidden darkness
   and suffer with us there.

6 Lord, if you now are risen,
   help all who long for light
   to hold the hand of promise
   and walk into the night.

B. Wren

43

1 Holy, holy, holy is the Lord;
   holy is the Lord God almighty!
   Jesus, Jesus, Jesus is the Lord;
   Jesus is the Lord God almighty,
   who was, and is, and is to come:
   holy, holy, holy is the Lord!

2 Worthy, worthy, worthy is the Lord;
   worthy is the Lord God almighty!
   Glory, glory, glory to the Lord;
   glory to the Lord God almighty,
   who was, and is, and is to come:
   holy, holy, holy is the Lord!

Anon.

44

How good it is to sing praise to our God!
The right and pleasant thing to praise his name.
The Lord is building up Jerusalem,
he gathers all the lost of Israel.
He is healing the broken-hearted, he is binding all their wounds,
he determines the stars in the heavens and he calls them each by name.
Great is the Lord in power, all things he knows,
he casts the wicked down, but lifts the low.

Psalm 147: 1—6
(New International Version)

45

POPULAR VERSION

1   How lovely on the mountains are the feet of him
    who brings good news, good news,
    proclaiming peace, announcing news of happiness:
    our God reigns, our God reigns!
      Our God reigns!   (4 times)

2   You watchmen lift your voices joyfully as one,
    shout for your king, your king.
    See eye to eye the Lord restoring Zion:
    your God reigns, your God reigns!
      Your God reigns!   (4 times)

3   Waste places of Jerusalem break forth with joy,
    we are redeemed, redeemed.
    The Lord has saved and comforted his people:
    your God reigns, your God reigns!

4   Ends of the earth, see the salvation of your God,
    Jesus is Lord, is Lord.
    Before the nations he has bared his holy arm:
    your God reigns, your God reigns!

ORIGINAL VERSION

1   How lovely on the mountains are the feet of him
    who brings good news, good news,
    proclaiming peace, announcing news of happiness:
    our God reigns, our God reigns!
      Our God reigns!   (4 times)

2 He had no stately form, he had no majesty,
that we should be drawn to him.
He was despised and we took no account of him,
yet now he reigns with the most high.
Now he reigns (3 times)
with the most high!

3 It was our sin and guilt that bruised and wounded him,
it was our sin that brought him down.
When we like sheep had gone astray, our shepherd came
and on his shoulders bore our shame.
On his shoulders (3 times)
he bore our shame.

4 Meek as a lamb that's led out to the slaughterhouse,
dumb as a sheep before its shearer,
his life ran down upon the ground like pouring rain,
that we might be born again.
That we might be (3 times)
born again.

5 Out from the tomb he came with grace and majesty,
he is alive, he is alive.
God loves us so — see here his hands, his feet, his side,
yes, we know he is alive.
He is alive! (4 times)

6 How lovely on the mountains are the feet of him
who brings good news, good news,
announcing peace, proclaiming news of happiness:
our God reigns, our God reigns.
Our God reigns! (4 times)

L. Smith Jnr.

46

1 Humbly in your sight we come together, Lord,
grant us now the blessing of your presence here.

2 These, our hearts, are yours, we give them to you, Lord,
purify our love to make it like your own.

3 These, our eyes, are yours, we give them to you, Lord,
may we always see your world as with your sight.

4 These, our hands, are yours, we give them to you, Lord,
give them strength and skill to do all work for you.

5 These, our feet, are yours, we give them to you, Lord,
may we always walk the path of life with you.

6 These, our tongues, are yours, we give them to you, Lord,
may we speak your healing words of life and truth.

7 These, our ears, are yours, we give them to you, Lord,
open them to hear the Gospel as from you.

8 Our whole selves are yours, we give them to you, Lord,
take us now and keep us yours for evermore.

Tumbuka hymn by J. Chirwa
translated and adapted by T. Colvin

47

1 I danced in the morning
when the world was begun,
and I danced in the moon
and the stars and the sun,
and I came down from heaven
and I danced on the earth —
at Bethlehem I had my birth.
Dance then wherever you may be,
I am the Lord of the Dance, said he,
and I'll lead you all, wherever you may be,
and I'll lead you all in the dance, said he.

2 I danced for the scribe
and the pharisee,
but they would not dance
and they wouldn't follow me,
I danced for the fishermen
for James and John —
they came with me
and the dance went on.

3 I danced on the Sabbath
and I cured the lame,
the holy people
said it was a shame.
They whipped and they stripped
and they hung me high,
and they left me there
on a cross to die.

4 I danced on a Friday
when the sky turned black —
it's hard to dance
with the devil on your back.
They buried my body
and they thought I'd gone —
but I am the dance
and I still go on.

5 They cut me down
and I leap up high —
I am the life
that'll never, never die.
I'll live in you
if you'll live in me,
I am the Lord
of the Dance, said he.

S. Carter

48

1 I need thee every hour,
most gracious Lord;
no tender voice but thine
can peace afford.
I need thee, O I need thee,
every hour I need thee;
O bless me now, my Saviour,
I come to thee.

2 I need thee every hour,
stay thou near by;
temptations lose their power
when thou art nigh.

3 I need thee every hour,
in joy or pain;
come quickly and abide,
or life is vain.

4 I need thee every hour,
teach me thy will;
and thy rich promises
in me fulfil.

A. Hawks

49

I will enter his gates with thanksgiving in my heart,
I will enter his courts with praise;
I will say this is the day that the Lord has made,
I will rejoice for he has made me glad.
He has made me glad, he has made me glad,
I will rejoice for he has made me glad.

Anon.

50

1 I will sing, I will sing a song unto the Lord, *(3 times)*
alleluia, glory to the Lord:
   Allelu, alleluia, glory to the Lord, (3 times)
   alleluia, glory to the Lord.

2 We will come, we will come as one before the Lord, *(3 times)*
alleluia, glory to the Lord!

3 If the Son, if the Son shall make you free, *(3 times)*
you shall be free indeed:

4 They that sow in tears shall reap in joy, *(3 times)*
allcluia, glory to the Lord!

M. Dyer

51

1 In a byre near Bethlehem,
  passed by many a wandering stranger,
  the most precious Word of Life
  was heard gurgling in a manger
  for the good of us all.
    And he's here when we call him,
    bringing health, love and laughter
    to life now and ever after
    for the good of us all.

2 By the Galilean Lake
  where the people flocked for teaching,
  the most precious Word of Life
  fed their mouths as well as preaching
  for the good of us all.

3 Quiet was Gethsemane,
  camouflaging priest and soldier,
  the most precious Word of Life
  took the world's weight on his shoulder
  for the good of us all.

4 On the hill of Calvary,
  place to end all hope of living,
  the most precious Word of Life
  breathed his last and died forgiving
  for the good of us all.

5 In a garden, just at dawn,
  near the grave of human violence,
  the most precious Word of Life
  cleared his throat and ended silence
  for the good of us all.

J. Bell and G. Maule

52

It's me, it's me, O Lord,
standing in the need of prayer.
It's me, it's me, O Lord,
standing in the need of prayer.

1 Not my mother or my father,
  but it's me, O Lord,
  standing in the need of prayer.
  Not my mother or my father,
  but it's me, O Lord,
  standing in the need of prayer.

2 Not my brother or my sister,
  but it's me, O Lord,
  standing in the need of prayer.
  Not my brother . . .

3 Not the stranger or the neighbour,
  but it's me, O Lord,
  standing in the need of prayer.
  Not the stranger . . .

Spiritual

53

1 It's no life, no life at all, that's rooted in deception,
  it's no life when human warmth is missing from perception.
  Living is a whole lot more than scrambling for survival,
  going through the motions with your neighbour as a rival.
  Jesus Christ, he is the life, he is the life of the world.

2 It's no life, no life at all, in slavery to suffer,
  with no shelter or a voice or money for a buffer.
  Living ought to be more like a wonderful adventure,
  with the freedom to move out in any kind of venture.

3 It's no life, no life at all, when there's no future showing,
memory is not enough to keep a person going.
Living cannot be reliving of the past, discouraged,
life must be attainable and real for hope to flourish.

4 It is life, authentic life, that Jesus has to offer,
working with us to transform our world where people suffer.
Tyranny shall be no more and all oppression vanish;
in his kingdom full of joy the fear of death is banished.

J. Maraschin tr. L. Lythgoe

54

1 Jesus calls us here to meet him
as, through word and song and prayer,
we affirm God's promised presence
where his people live and care.
Praise the God who keeps his promise;
praise the Son who calls us friends;
praise the Spirit who, among us,
to our hopes and fears attends.

2 Jesus calls us to confess him
Word of Life and Lord of all,
sharer of our flesh and frailness
saving all who fail or fall.
Tell his holy human story;
tell his tales that all may hear;
tell the world that Christ in glory
came to earth to meet us here.

3 Jesus calls us to each other:
found in him are no divides.
Race and class and sex and language:
such are barriers he derides.
Join the hand of friend and stranger;
join the hands of age and youth;
join the faithful and the doubter
in their common search for truth.

4 Jesus calls us to his table
rooted firm in time and space,
where the church in earth and heaven
finds a common meeting place.
Share the bread and wine, his body;
share the love of which we sing;
share the feast for saints and sinners
hosted by our Lord and King.

J. Bell and G. Maule

55

1 Jesus is Lord! Creation's voice proclaims it,
  for by his power each tree and flower was planned and made.
  Jesus is Lord! The universe declares it,
  sun, moon and stars in heaven cry Jesus is Lord!
  Jesus is Lord! Jesus is Lord!
  Praise him with hallelujahs, for Jesus is Lord!

2 Jesus is Lord! Yet from his throne eternal
  in flesh he came to die in pain on Calvary's tree.
  Jesus is Lord! From him all life proceeding,
  yet gave his life a ransom thus setting us free.

3 Jesus is Lord! O'er sin the mighty conqueror,
  from death he rose and all his foes shall own his name.
  Jesus is Lord! God sends his Holy Spirit
  to show by works of power that Jesus is Lord.

D. Mansell

56

1 Jesus, stand among us at the meeting of our lives,
  be our sweet agreement at the meeting of our eyes;
  O, Jesus, we love you, so we gather here,
  join our hearts in unity and take away our fear.

2 So to you we're gathering out of each and every land,
  Christ the love between us at the joining of our hands;

G. Kendrick

57

1 Jesus the Lord said: 'I am the Bread,
  the Bread of Life for mankind am I,
  the Bread of Life for mankind am I,
  the Bread of Life for mankind am I.'
  Jesus the Lord said: 'I am the Bread,
  the Bread of Life for mankind am I.'

2 Jesus the Lord said: 'I am the Door,
  the Way and the Door for the poor am I.' ...

3 Jesus the Lord said: 'I am the Light,
  the one true Light of the world am I.' ...

4 Jesus the Lord said: 'I am the Shepherd,
the one Good Shepherd of the sheep am I.' ...

5 Jesus the Lord said: 'I am the Life,
the Resurrection and the Life am I.' ...

translated from the Urdu by D. Monahan

58

Jubilate Deo, jubilate Deo, alleluia.

(O praise God, praise God, alleluia.)

59

Jubilate, everybody,
serve the Lord in all your ways,
and come before his presence singing,
enter now his courts with praise.
For the Lord our God is gracious,
and his mercy everlasting.
Jubilate, jubilate, jubilate Deo!

Psalm 100 tr. F. Dunn

60

1 Kneels at the feet of his friends,
silently washes their feet,
master who acts as a slave to them.
Jesu, Jesu,
fill us with your love,
show us how to serve
the neighbours we have
from you.

2 Neighbours are rich folk and poor,
neighbours are black, brown, and white,
neighbours are nearby and far away.

3 These are the ones we should serve,
these are the ones we should love,
all these are neighbours to us and you.

4 Loving puts us on our knees,
 serving as though we were slaves,
 this is the way we should live with you.

5 Kneel at the feet of our friends,
 silently washing their feet,
 this is the way we should live with you.

T. Colvin

61

Kyrie eleison.

(Lord, have mercy.)

62

1 Lead us, O Father, in the paths of peace:
 without thy guiding hand we go astray,
 and doubts appal, and sorrows still increase;
 lead us through Christ, the true and living Way.

2 Lead us, O Father, in the paths of truth:
 unhelped by thee, in error's maze we grope,
 while passion stains and folly dims our youth,
 and age comes on uncheered by faith or hope.

3 Lead us, O Father, in the paths of right:
 blindly we stumble when we walk alone,
 involved in shadows of a darkening night;
 only with thee we journey safely on.

4 Lead us, O Father, to thy heavenly rest,
 however rough and steep the pathway be,
 through joy or sorrow, as thou deemest best,
 until our lives are perfected in thee.

W. Burleigh

63

1 Let the world unite and sing
 praises to our glorious King:
 Alleluya, alleluya to our King.

2 Of his power and glory tell,
   all his work he does so well.

3 Come, and see what he has done,
   deeds of wonder every one.

4 You who fear him now draw near,
   praise our God who holds you dear.

5 Let us all together sing
   praises to our glorious King:

Malawi hymn
translated by H. Taylor
adapted by T. Colvin

64

Solo   Let us go to the house of the Lord.
All 1 I rejoiced with those who said to me, Let us go to the house of the
   Lord.
   Our feet are standing in your gates, Jerusalem,
   like a city built together, where the people of God go up
   to praise the name of the Lord.

2 For peace for our Jerusalem and loved ones this we pray:
   may your folk be secure where they must live,
   and to all God's friends and family may the peace be within you,
   for the sake of the house of the Lord.

From Psalm 122
(New International Version)

65

1 Let us talents and tongues employ,
   reaching out with a shout of joy:
   bread is broken, wine is poured,
   Christ is spoken and seen and heard:
      Jesus lives again, earth can breathe again,
      pass the word around: loaves abound.

2 Christ is able to make us one,
   at his table he sets the tone,
   teaching people to live to bless,
   love in word and in deed express:

3 Jesus calls us in, sends us out
   bearing fruit in a world of doubt,
   gives us love to tell, bread to share:
   God-Immanuel everywhere:

                              F. Kaan

66

Lifted high on your cross,
drawing all folk, drawing all folk;
lifted high on your cross,
drawing all folk to you.

1 Down you come to live among us
   part of your creation,
   knowing poverty and sorrow,
   sharing each temptation.

2 On the gallows there they nail you
   God despised, rejected,
   deep within your earth they hide you
   till you're resurrected.

3 Light and love pour down upon us,
   healing, recreating,
   you re-live your life within us,
   all life consecrating.

                              I. Cowie

67

1 Like a sea without a shore
   love divine is boundless.
   Time is now and evermore
   and his love surrounds us.
     Maranatha! Maranatha!
     Maranatha! Come, Lord Jesus, come!

2 So that mankind could be free
   he appeared among us.
   Blest are those who have not seen
   yet believe his promise.

3 All our visions, all our dreams,
   are but ghostly shadows
   of the radiant clarity
   waiting at life's close.

4 Death where is your victory?
   Death where is your sting?
   Closer than the air we breathe
   is our risen King.

E. White

(*Maranatha* is an Aramaic phrase meaning 'Lord, come!'
See 1 Corinthians 16:22.)

68

1 Living under the shadow of his wing
   we find security.
   Standing in his presence we will bring
   our worship, worship, worship to the King.

2 Bowed in adoration at his feet,
   we dwell in harmony,
   voices joined together that repeat,
   worthy, worthy, worthy is the Lord.

3 Heart to heart embracing in his love,
   reveals his purity,
   soaring in my spirit like a dove,
   holy, holy, holy is the Lord.

D. Hadden and R. Silvester

69

1 Look forward in faith —
   all time is in God's hand.
   Walk humbly with him
   and trust his future plan.
   God has wisely led
   his people by his power.
   Look forward in hope,
   he gives us each new hour.

2 Look forward in faith —
   the world is in God's care.
   His purpose of love
   he calls on us to share.
   In our neighbour's need,
   the Lord is present still.
   He blesses the meek!
   The earth will know God's will.

3 Look forward in faith —
   God gives us life each day.
   Go onward with Christ,
   his Spirit guides our way.
   Now God lets us live
   within the sphere of grace.
   Trust ever in him —
   he rules o'er earth and space!

                                    A. Scobie

70

1 Lord, bring the day to pass
   when forest, rock and hill,
   the beasts, the birds, the grass,
   will know your finished will,
   when we attain our destiny
   and nature lives in harmony.

2 Forgive our careless use
   of water, ore and soil —
   the plenty we abuse
   supplied by others' toil:
   save us from making self our creed,
   turn us towards each other's need.

3 Give us, when we release
   creation's secret powers,
   to harness them for peace,
   our children's peace and ours:
   teach us the art of mastering
   in servant form, which draws death's sting.

4 Creation groans, travails,
   futile its present plight,
   bound — till the hour it hails
   God's children born of light
   who enter on their true estate.
   Come, Lord: new heavens and earth create.

                                    I. Fraser

71

1 Lord God, your love has called us here
   as we, by love, for love were made.
   Your living likeness still we bear,
   though marred, dishonoured, disobeyed.
   We come, with all our heart and mind
   your call to hear, your love to find.

2 We come with self-inflicted pains
of broken trust and chosen wrong,
half-free, half-bound by inner chains,
by social forces swept along,
by powers and systems close confined
yet seeking hope for humankind.

3 Lord God, in Christ you call our name
and then receive us as your own,
not through some merit, right or claim,
but by your gracious love alone.
We strain to glimpse your mercy-seat
and find you kneeling at our feet.

4 Then take the towel, and break the bread,
and humble us, and call us friends.
Suffer and serve till all are fed,
and show how grandly love intends
to work till all creation sings,
to fill all worlds, to crown all things.

5 Lord God, in Christ you set us free
your life to live, your joy to share.
Give us your Spirit's liberty
to turn from guilt and dull despair
and offer all that faith can do
while love is making all things new.

B. Wren

72

1 Lord Jesus Christ, you have come to us,
you are one with us, Mary's son —
cleansing our souls from all their sin,
pouring your love and goodness in;
Jesus, our love for you we sing, living Lord.

2 Lord Jesus Christ, now and every day
teach us how to pray, Son of God.
You have commanded us to do
this, in remembrance, Lord, of you;
into our lives your power breaks through, living Lord.

3 Lord Jesus Christ, you have come to us,
born as one of us, Mary's son —
led out to die on Calvary,
risen from death to set us free;
living Lord Jesus, help us see you are Lord.

4 Lord Jesus Christ, we would come to you,
live our lives for you, Son of God;
all your commands we know are true;
your many gifts will make us new;
into our lives your power breaks through, living Lord.

P. Appleford

73

1 Lord of life, so many joys
and blessings fill our days.
Lord, to you we offer thanks
and sing our song of praise.
Music, light and laughter come
as gifts which show your love.
Lord of life, our happy days
your grace and goodness prove.

2 Lord of life, this world is yours —
the sweep of sea and land;
and every living cell proclaims
a great creator's hand.
Summer flowers and autumn fruits,
reserves of wealth and power;
nature's bounty is your gift
for humankind to share.

3 Lord of life, your greatest gift
is Christ, in whom we see
the heart of all you plan for us,
our human destiny.
In perfect love he lived on earth,
showed us your truth and way,
and life abundant gives to all
who follow him today.

A. Scobie

74

Lord, to whom shall we go?
Yours are the words of eternal life.

John 6: 68

75

Majesty, worship his majesty;
unto Jesus be glory, honour and praise.
Majesty, kingdom, authority
flows from his throne unto his own, his anthem raise.
So exalt, lift up on high the name of Jesus,
magnify, come glorify Christ Jesus the King.
Majesty, worship his majesty,
Jesus who died, now glorified, king of all kings.

J. Hayford

76

1 Make me a channel of your peace.
   Where there is hatred let me bring your love;
   where there is injury, your pardon, Lord;
   and where there's doubt, true faith in you.
   Oh, master, grant that I may never seek
   so much to be consoled as to console;
   to be understood as to understand;
   to be loved, as to love with all my soul.

2 Make me a channel of your peace.
   Where there's despair in life let me bring hope;
   where there is darkness, only light;
   and where there's sadness, ever joy.

3 Make me a channel of your peace.
   It is in pardoning that we are pardoned,
   in giving to all men that we receive;
   and in dying that we're born to eternal life. *(no refrain)*

S. Temple
(from the Prayer of St Francis)

77

1 Many are the lightbeams from the one light.
   Our one light is Jesus.
   Many are the lightbeams from the one light;
   we are one in Christ.

2 Many are the branches of the one tree.
   Our one tree is Jesus.
   Many are the branches of the one tree;
   we are one in Christ.

3 Many are the gifts given, love is all one.
   Love's the gift of Jesus.
   Many are the gifts given, love is all one;
   we are one in Christ.

4 Many ways to serve God, the Spirit is one;
   servant spirit of Jesus.
   Many ways to serve God, the Spirit is one;
   we are one in Christ.

5 Many are the members, the body is one;
  members all of Jesus.
  Many are the members, the body is one;
  we are one in Christ.

A. Frostenson, translated by D. Lewis

78

1 Morning has broken
  like the first morning;
  blackbird has spoken
  like the first bird.
  Praise for the singing!
  Praise for the morning!
  Praise for them, springing
  fresh from the Word!

2 Sweet the rain's new fall
  sunlit from heaven,
  like the first dewfall
  on the first grass.
  Praise for the sweetness
  of the wet garden,
  sprung in completeness
  where his feet pass.

3 Mine is the sunlight!
  Mine is the morning
  born of the one light
  Eden saw play!
  Praise with elation,
  praise every morning,
  God's re-creation
  of the new day!

E. Farjeon

79

Nada te turbe, nada te espante:
quien a Dios tiene nada le falta.
Nada te turbe, nada te espante:
sólo Dios basta.

(Let nothing worry or upset you:
whoever has God needs fear nothing.
Let nothing worry or upset you:
God alone is enough.)

From the Taizé Community

80

Solo   1   Night has fallen,
All   night has fallen.
God our maker,
guard us sleeping.

Solo   2   Darkness now has come,
All   darkness now has come.

Solo   3   We are with you, Lord,
All   we are with you, Lord.

Solo   4   You have kept us, Lord,
All   you have kept us, Lord.

Solo   5   See your children, Lord,
All   see your children, Lord.

Solo   6   Keep us in your love,
All   keep us in your love.

Solo   7   Now we go to rest,
All   now we go to rest.

Chewa Hymn, translated by T. Colvin

81

1 Now through the grace of God we claim
   this life to be his own,
   baptised with water in the name
   of Father, Spirit, Son.

2 For Jesus Christ the crucified,
   who broke the power of sin,
   now lives to plead for those baptised
   in unity with him.

3 So let us act upon his word,
   rejoicing in our faith,
   until we rise with Christ our Lord
   and triumph over death!

M. Perry

82

1 O Christ, the healer, we have come
   to pray for health, to plead for friends.
   How can we fail to be restored,
   when reached by love that never ends?

2 From every ailment flesh endures
  our bodies clamour to be freed;
  yet in our hearts we would confess
  that wholeness is our deepest need.

3 How strong, O Lord, are our desires,
  how weak our knowledge of ourselves!
  Release in us those healing truths
  unconscious pride resists or shelves.

4 In conflicts that destroy our health
  we diagnose the world's disease:
  our common life declares our ills:
  is there no cure, O Christ, for these?

5 Grant that we all, made one in faith,
  in your community may find
  the wholeness that, enriching us,
  shall reach the whole of humankind.

F. Pratt Green

83

1 O happy day, that fixed my choice
  on thee, my Saviour and my God!
  Well may this glowing heart rejoice,
  and tell its raptures all abroad.
    Happy day! happy day! when Jesus washed my sins away!
    He taught me how to watch and pray,
    and live rejoicing every day;
    Happy day! happy day! when Jesus washed my sins away!

2 'Tis done, the great transaction's done!
  I am my Lord's, and he is mine.
  He drew me, and I followed on,
  charmed to confess the voice divine.

3 Now rest, my long-divided heart,
  fixed on this blissful centre, rest;
  nor ever from thy Lord depart,
  with him of every good possessed.

4 High heaven, that heard the solemn vow,
  that vow renewed shall daily hear,
  till in life's latest hour I bow,
  and bless in death a bond so dear.

P. Doddridge

84

1 O Lord, all the world belongs to you,
   and you are always making all things new.
   What is wrong you forgive,
   and the new life you give
   is what's turning the world upside down.

2 The world's only loving to its friends,
   but your way of loving never ends,
   loving enemies too;
   and this loving with you,
   is what's turning the world upside down.

3 The world lives divided and apart,
   you draw us together, and we start
   in our friendship to see
   that in harmony we
   can be turning the world upside down.

4 The world wants the wealth to live in state,
   but you show a new way to be great:
   like a servant you came,
   and if we do the same,
   we'll be turning the world upside down.

5 O Lord, all the world belongs to you,
   and you are always making all things new.
   What is wrong you forgive,
   and the new life you give
   is what's turning the world upside down.

P. Appleford

85

O Lord hear my prayer, O Lord hear my prayer:
when I call answer me.
O Lord hear my prayer, O Lord hear my prayer:
come and listen to me.
(repeat)

From the Taizé Community

86

1 O Lord my God! when I in awesome wonder
consider all the works thy hand hath made,
I see the stars, I hear the mighty thunder,
thy power throughout the universe displayed:
Then sings my soul, my Saviour God, to thee,
how great thou art, how great thou art!
Then sings my soul, my Saviour God, to thee,
how great thou art, how great thou art!

2 When through the woods and forest glades I wander
and hear the birds sing sweetly in the trees;
when I look down from lofty mountain grandeur,
and hear the brook, and feel the gentle breeze:

3 And when I think that God his Son not sparing,
sent him to die — I scarce can take it in,
that on the cross my burden gladly bearing,
he bled and died to take away my sin:

4 When Christ shall come with shout of acclamation
and take me home — what joy shall fill my heart!
Then shall I bow in humble adoration
and there proclaim, my God, how great thou art!

Russian hymn
translated by S. Hine

87

1 Oh the life of the world is a joy and a treasure,
unfolding in beauty the green-growing tree,
the changing of seasons in mountain and valley,
the stars and the bright restless sea.

2 Oh the life of the world is a fountain of goodness
overflowing in labour and passion and pain,
in the sound of the city and the silence of wisdom,
in the birth of a child once again.

3 Oh the life of the world is the source of our healing.
It rises in laughter and wells up in song;
it springs from the care of the poor and the broken
and refreshes where justice is strong.

4 So give thanks for the life and give love to the maker,
and rejoice in the gift of the bright risen Son,
and walk in the peace and the power of the Spirit
till the days of our living are done.

K. Galloway

88

O what a gift, what a wonderful gift!
Who can tell the wonders of the Lord?
Let us open our eyes, our ears, and our hearts;
it is Christ the Lord, it is he!

1 In the stillness of the night when the world was asleep,
the almighty Word leapt out.
He came to Mary, he came to us,
Christ came to the land of Galilee.
Christ our Lord and our King!

2 On the night before he died it was passover night,
and he gathered his friends together.
He broke the bread, he blessed the wine;
it was the gift of his love and his life.
Christ our Lord and our King!

3 On the hill of Calvary the world held its breath,
for there for the world to see,
God gave his Son, his very own Son,
for the love of you and me.
Christ our Lord and our King!

4 Early on that morning when the world was sleeping,
back to life came he!
He conquered death, he conquered sin,
but the victory he gave to you and me!
Christ our Lord and our King!

5 Some day with the saints we will come before our Father
and then we will shout and dance and sing.
For in our midst for our eyes to see
will be Christ our Lord and our King.
Christ our Lord and our King!

P. Howard

89

1 Oh, the love of my Lord is the essence
of all that I love here on earth.
All the beauty I see
he has given to me
and his giving is gentle as silence.

2 Every day, every hour, every moment
has been blessed by the strength of his love.
At the turn of each tide
he is there at my side,
and his touch is as gentle as silence.

3 There've been times when I've turned from his presence,
and I've walked other paths, other ways.
But I've called on his name
in the dark of my shame,
and his mercy was gentle as silence.

E. White

90

1 One more step along the world I go,
one more step along the world I go;
from the old things to the new
keep me travelling along with you:
   And it's from the old I travel to the new;
   keep me travelling along with you.

2 Round the corner of the world I turn,
more and more about the world I learn;
all the new things that I see
you'll be looking at along with me:

3 As I travel through the bad and good,
keep me travelling the way I should;
where I see no way to go
you'll be telling me the way, I know:

4 Give me courage when the world is rough,
keep me loving though the world is tough;
leap and sing in all I do,
keep me travelling along with you:

5 You are older than the world can be,
 you are younger than the life in me;
 ever old and ever new,
 keep me travelling along with you:

S. Carter

91

1 Our Lord Christ hath risen! The tempter is foiled;
 his legions are scattered, his strongholds are spoiled.
   O sing hallelujah, O sing hallelujah,
   O sing hallelujah! Be joyful and sing,
   Our great foe is baffled — Christ Jesus is King!

2 O death, we defy thee! A stronger than thou
 hath entered thy palace; we fear thee not now!
   O sing hallelujah, O sing hallelujah,
   O sing hallelujah! Be joyful and sing,
   Death cannot affright us — Christ Jesus is King!

3 O sin, thou art vanquished, thy long reign is o'er;
 though still thou dost vex us, we dread thee no more.
   O sing hallelujah, O sing hallelujah,
   O sing hallelujah! Be joyful and sing,
   Who now can condemn us? Christ Jesus is King!

4 Our Lord Christ hath risen! Day breaketh at last;
 the long night of weeping is now well-nigh past.
   O sing hallelujah, O sing hallelujah,
   O sing hallelujah! Be joyful and sing,
   Our foes are all conquered — Christ Jesus is King!

W. Plunket

92

1 Praise the Lord, all ye servants of the Lord,
 who minister by night within his house.
 Lift up your hands within the sanctuary,
 and praise the Lord.

2 May this Lord, the maker of heaven and earth,
   may this Lord bless you from Zion.
   Lift up your hands within the sanctuary,
   and praise the Lord.

From Psalm 134
(New International Version)

93

1 Seek ye first the kingdom of God
   and his righteousness;
   and all these things shall be added unto you;
   allelu, alleluia.
        Alleluia, alleluia, alleluia, alleluia!

2 Ask, and it shall be given unto you,
   seek, and ye shall find;
   knock, and the door shall be opened unto you;
   allelu, alleluia.

3 Man shall not live by bread alone,
   but by every word
   that proceeds from the mouth of the Lord;
   allelu, alleluia.

K. Lafferty

94

1 Sing alleluia to the Lord,
   sing alleluia to the Lord,
   sing alleluia, sing alleluia,
   sing alleluia to the Lord!

2 Jesus is risen from the dead,
   Jesus is risen from the dead,
   Jesus is risen, Jesus is risen,
   Jesus is risen from the dead!

3 Jesus is Lord of heaven and earth,
   Jesus is Lord of heaven and earth,
   Jesus is Lord, Jesus is Lord,
   Jesus is Lord of heaven and earth!

v. 1: L. Stassen
vv. 2 & 3: Anon.

95

1 Sing of the Lord's goodness, Father of all wisdom,
come to him and bless his name.
Mercy he has shown us, his love is for ever,
faithful to the end of days.
   Come then all you nations, sing of your Lord's goodness,
   melodies of praise and thanks to God.
   Ring out the Lord's glory, praise him with your music,
   worship him and bless his name.

2 Power he has wielded, honour is his garment,
risen from the snares of death.
His word he has spoken, one bread he has broken,
new life he now gives to all.

3 Courage in our darkness, comfort in our sorrow,
Spirit of our God most high;
solace for the weary, pardon for the sinner,
splendour of the living God.

4 Praise him with your singing, praise him with the trumpet,
praise God with the lute and harp;
praise him with the cymbals, praise him with your dancing,
praise God till the end of days.

E. Sands

96

1 Sing we a song of high revolt —
make great the Lord, his name exalt:
sing we the song that Mary sang,
of God at war with human wrong.

2 Sing we of him who deeply cares,
and still with us our burden bears;
he who with strength the proud disowns,
brings down the mighty from their thrones.

3 By him the poor are lifted up —
he satisfies with bread and cup
the hungry folk of many lands;
the rich must go with empty hands.

4 He calls us to revolt and fight
   with him for what is just and right;
   to sing and live 'Magnificat'
   in crowded street and council flat.

F. Kaan

97

1 Sons and daughters of creation,
   by God's will we come to be;
   like a poet dreaming marvels
   he has spun our history,
   working, till from shapeless chaos,
   he evoked humanity.

2 Dark within our first conceiving
   run the rifts that still divide.
   Envy splits and anger hardens;
   colour, gender, wealth collide;
   sovereign nations arm for conflict
   violence thrusting peace aside.

3 Yet God holds his steadfast purpose
   of humanity made one.
   Walls were breached and bounds transcended
   by the death of his own Son;
   and the way of love's encounter
   through the Spirit's power begun.

4 Down the restless generations,
   called of God, his Church has grown;
   martyrs, heirs and prophets' children
   penetrated lands unknown;
   Christians challenged by unlikeness,
   finding gifts to aid their own.

5 Now as partners in one mission,
   we must share across the earth
   hope of what God will accomplish,
   faith that promises new birth
   to the selves that sin has shattered,
   love restoring human worth.

6 Rich from all that we inherit,
  strong with skills new worlds devise,
  Father, may we serve your kingdom
  under crisis-clouded skies,
  confidently re-affirming
  where the morning's glory lies.

Anon.

98

Spirit of the living God, fall afresh on me,
Spirit of the living God, fall afresh on me:
break me, melt me, mould me, fill me.
Spirit of the living God, fall afresh on me.

D. Iverson

99

Stay with me, remain here with me.
Watch and pray, watch and pray.

From the Taizé Community

100

Surrexit Dominus vere,
Alleluia, alleluia.
Surrexit Christus hodie,
Alleluia, alleluia.

Alternative English words:
Jesus, the Lord, has risen,
Alleluia, alleluia.
Christ is alive for ever,
Alleluia, alleluia.

From the Taizé Community

101

The God of heaven is present on earth
in word and silence and sharing,
in face of doubt, in depth of faith,
in signs of love and caring.

1 Gentler than air, wilder than wind,
   settling yet also deranging,
   the Spirit thrives in human lives
   both changeless and yet changing.

2 Far from the church, outside the fold,
   where prayer turns feeble and nervous,
   the Spirit wills society's ills
   be healed through humble service.

3 From country quiet to city riot,
   in every human confusion,
   the Spirit pleads for all that leads
   to freedom from illusion.

4 Truth after tears, trust after fears,
   God after all that denies him:
   the Spirit springs through hopeless things
   transforming what defies him.

J. Bell and G. Maule

102

1 The Spirit lives to set us free,
   walk, walk in the light.
   He binds us all in unity,
   walk, walk in the light.
   Walk in the light,
   walk in the light,
   walk in the light,
   walk in the light of the Lord.

2 Jesus promised life to all,
   walk, walk in the light.
   The dead were wakened by his call,
   walk, walk in the light.

3 He died in pain on Calvary,
   walk, walk in the light,
   to save the lost like you and me,
   walk, walk in the light.

4 We know his death was not the end,
   walk, walk in the light.
   He gave his Spirit to be our friend,
   walk, walk in the light.

5 By Jesus' love our wounds are healed,
walk, walk in the light.
The Father's kindness is revealed,
walk, walk in the light.

6 The Spirit lives in you and me,
walk, walk in the light.
His light will shine for all to see,
walk, walk in the light.

D. Lundy

103

1 The voice of God goes out to all the world;
his glory speaks across the universe.
The great King's herald cries from star to star:
with power, with justice, he will walk his way.

2 The Lord has said: 'Receive my messenger,
my promise to the world, my pledge made flesh,
a lamp to every nation, light from light':
with power, with justice, he will walk his way.

3 The broken reed he will not trample down,
nor set his heel upon the dying flame.
He binds the wounds, and health is in his hand:
with power, with justice, he will walk his way.

4 Anointed with the Spirit and with power,
he comes to crown with comfort all the weak,
to show the face of justice to the poor:
with power, with justice, he will walk his way.

5 His touch will bless the eyes that darkness held,
the lame shall run, the halting tongue shall sing,
and prisoners laugh in light and liberty:
with power, with justice, he will walk his way.

P. Icarus

104

1 There's a spirit in the air,
telling Christians everywhere:
praise the love that Christ revealed,
living, working, in our world.

2 Lose your shyness, find your tongue;
   tell the world what God has done:
   God in Christ has come to stay;
   live tomorrow's life today!

3 When believers break the bread,
   when a hungry child is fed,
   praise the love that Christ revealed,
   living, working, in our world.

4 Still the Spirit gives us light,
   seeing wrong and setting right:
   God in Christ has come to stay;
   live tomorrow's life today!

5 When a stranger's not alone,
   where the homeless find a home,
   praise the love that Christ revealed,
   living, working, in our world.

6 May the Spirit fill our praise,
   guide our thoughts and change our ways:
   God in Christ has come to stay;
   live tomorrow's life today!

7 There's a Spirit in the air,
   calling people everywhere:
   praise the love that Christ revealed,
   living, working, in our world.

                                    B. Wren

105

1 This is the day,
   this is the day that the Lord has made,
   that the Lord has made.
   We will rejoice,
   we will rejoice and be glad in it,
   and be glad in it.
   This is the day that the Lord has made,
   we will rejoice and be glad in it.
   This is the day,
   this is the day that the Lord has made.

2 This is the day . . . that he rose again,

3 This is the day . . . when the Spirit came,

                                    Anon.

106

1 Those who wait on the Lord shall renew their strength,
  they shall rise up on wings as eagles,
  they shall run and not be weary, they shall walk and not faint:
  help us Lord, help us Lord in your way.

2 Those who serve the suffering world shall renew their strength,

3 Those who live the risen life shall renew their strength,

4 Those who love the Mystery shall renew their strength,

5 Those who die on the march shall renew their strength,

6 Those who wait on the Lord shall renew their strength,

107

1 Through the love of God our Saviour
  all will be well.
  Free and changeless is his favour;
  all, all is well.
  Precious is the blood that healed us,
  perfect is the grace that sealed us,
  strong the hand stretched forth to shield us;
  all must be well.

2 Though we pass through tribulation,
  all will be well.
  Ours is such a full salvation,
  all, all is well.
  Happy still in God confiding,
  fruitful, if in Christ abiding,
  holy, through the Spirit's guiding;
  all must be well.

3 We expect a bright to-morrow;
  all will be well.
  Faith can sing through days of sorrow,
  'All, all is well.'
  On our Father's love relying,
  Jesus every need supplying,
  or in living or in dying,
  all must be well.

M. Peters

108

Thuma mina Somandla

Solo	1	Send me, Lord.
All		Send me, Jesus, send me, Jesus, send me, Jesus, send me, Lord.

Solo	2	Lead me, Lord.
All		Lead me, Jesus, lead me, Jesus, lead me, Jesus, lead me, Lord.

Solo	3	Fill me, Lord.
All		Fill me, Jesus, fill me, Jesus, fill me, Jesus, fill me, Lord.

South African traditional hymn

109

Ubi caritas et amor,
ubi caritas, Deus ibi est.

*(Where there is charity and love,
God is there.)*

From the Taizé Community

110

We are marching in the light of God, *(etc.)*

South African traditional hymn

111

1 We are one in the Spirit,
  we are one in the Lord,
  we are one in the Spirit,
  we are one in the Lord,
  and we pray that all unity
  may one day be restored.
  *And they'll know we are Christians
  by our love, by our love,
  yes, they'll know we are Christians by our love.*

2 We will walk with each other,
  we will walk hand in hand,
  we will walk with each other,
  we will walk hand in hand.
  And together we'll spread the news
  that God is in our land.

3 We will work with each other,
  we will work side by side,
  we will work with each other,
  we will work side by side.
  And we'll guard each one's dignity
  and save each one's pride.

4 All praise to the Father
  from whom all things come,
  and all praise to Christ Jesus
  his only Son,
  and all praise to the Spirit
  who makes us one.

P. Scholtes

112

1 We cannot measure how you heal
  or answer every sufferer's prayer,
  yet we believe your grace responds
  where faith and doubt unite to care.

2 Your hands, though bloodied on the cross,
  survive to hold and heal and warn,
  to carry all through death to life
  and cradle children yet unborn.

3 The pain that will not go away,
  the guilt that clings from things long past,
  the fear of what the future holds
  are present as if meant to last.

4 But present too is love which tends
  the hurt we never hoped to find,
  the private agonies inside,
  the memories that haunt the mind.

5 So some have come who need your help
and some have come to make amends
as hands which shaped and saved the world
are present in the touch of friends.

6 Lord, let your Spirit meet us here
to mend the body, mind and soul,
to disentangle peace from pain
and make your broken people whole.

J. Bell and G. Maule

113

1 We lay our broken world
in sorrow at your feet,
haunted by hunger, war and fear,
oppressed by power and hate.

2 Here human life seems less
than profit, might and pride,
though to unite us all in you,
you lived and loved and died.

3 We bring our broken towns
our neighbours hurt and bruised;
you show us how old pain and wounds
for new life can be used.

4 We bring our broken loves,
friends parted, families torn;
then in your life and death we see
that love must be reborn.

5 We bring our broken selves,
confused and closed and tired;
then through your gift of healing grace
new purpose is inspired.

6 O Spirit, on us breathe,
with life and strength anew;
find in us love, and hope, and trust,
and lift us up to you.

A. Briggs

114

1 Were you there when they crucified my Lord?
Were you there when they crucified my Lord?
Oh! Sometimes it causes me to tremble, tremble, tremble;
were you there when they crucified my Lord?

2 Were you there when they nailed him to the tree? ...

3 Were you there when they laid him in the tomb? ...

4 Were you there when God raised him from the dead? ...

Spiritual

115

1 What a friend we have in Jesus,
all our sins and griefs to bear!
What a privilege to carry
everything to God in prayer!
O what peace we often forfeit,
O what needless pain we bear,
all because we do not carry
everything to God in prayer!

2 Have we trials and temptations?
Is there trouble anywhere?
We should never be discouraged:
take it to the Lord in prayer!
Can we find a friend so faithful,
who will all our sorrows share?
Jesus knows our every weakness:
take it to the Lord in prayer.

3 Are we weak and heavy-laden,
cumbered with a load of care?
Jesus is our only refuge:
take it to the Lord in prayer.
Do thy friends despise, forsake thee?
Take it to the Lord in prayer;
In his arms he'll take and shield thee;
thou wilt find a solace there.

J. Scriven

116

1 When our confidence is shaken
in beliefs we thought secure;
when the spirit in its sickness
seeks but cannot find a cure:
God is active in the tensions
of a faith not yet mature.

2 Solar systems, void of meaning,
freeze the spirit into stone;
always our researches lead us
to the ultimate unknown:
faith must die, or come full circle
to its source in God alone.

3 In the discipline of praying,
when it's hardest to believe;
in the drudgery of caring,
when it's not enough to grieve:
faith, maturing, learns acceptance
of the insights we receive.

4 God is love; and he redeems us
in the Christ we crucify:
this is God's eternal answer
to the world's eternal why;
may we in this faith maturing
be content to live and die!

F. Pratt Green

117

1 When our lives are joined to Christ
a new world comes to birth,
all the past already gone,
God's order here on earth.
From the first to last of time
this has been God's work of grace,
making enemies his friends —
a new world has begun!

2 In the life of Christ on earth
God came to us in love;
one man died that all might live,
our faults were far removed.
We are called in Jesus' name,
who was innocent of sin,
now to hear the word of peace —
a new world has begun!

3 Now in union with our Lord,
who conquers death and fear,
we may live at one with God
and in his goodness share.
He who gave the earth its birth
calls us still to work with him;
God's deliverance has dawned —
a new world has begun!

A. Scobie, paraphrased from 2 Corinthians 5: 17—6: 2

118

1 Will you come and follow me,
if I but call your name?
Will you go where you don't know
and never be the same?
Will you let my love be shown,
will you let my name be known,
will you let my life be grown
in you and you in me?

2 Will you leave your self behind
  if I but call your name?
  Will you care for cruel and kind
  and never be the same?
  Will you risk the hostile stare
  should your life attract or scare,
  will you let me answer prayer
  in you and you in me?

3 Will you let the blinded see
  if I but call your name?
  Will you set the prisoners free
  and never be the same?
  Will you kiss the leper clean
  and do such as this unseen,
  and admit to what I mean
  in you and you in me?

4 Will you love the 'you' you hide
  if I but call your name?
  Will you quell the fear inside
  and never be the same?
  Will you use the faith you've found
  to reshape the world around
  through my sight and touch and sound
  in you and you in me?

5 Lord, your summons echoes true
  when you but call my name.
  Let me turn and follow you
  and never be the same.
  In your company I'll go
  where your love and footsteps show.
  Thus I'll move and live and grow
  in you and you in me.

J. Bell and G. Maule

119

1 You are worthy, you are worthy,
  you are worthy, O Lord;
  you are worthy to receive glory,
  glory and honour and power:
  for you have created, have all things created,
  for you have created all things;
  and for your pleasure they are created;
  you are worthy, O Lord!

2 You are worthy, you are worthy,
   you are worthy, O Son;
   you are worthy to receive glory
   and praise in the midst of mankind:
   for you are the one who was born of a virgin,
   your life bringing light to the world;
   we bow down before you, love and adore you
   our Saviour, incarnate for all.

3 You are worthy, you are worthy,
   you are worthy, O Lamb;
   you are worthy to receive glory
   and power at the Father's right hand:
   for you have redeemed us, have ransomed and cleansed us,
   by your blood making us new;
   in white robes arrayed us, kings and priests made us
   and we are reigning in you.

4 You are worthy, you are worthy,
   you are worthy, O Lord;
   you are worthy to receive glory
   and praise at your coming to reign.
   You are the first of a new generation,
   the first to rise up from the dead;
   we bring you the praise of the whole of creation
   which waits for you, Jesus our Head.

P. Mills,
vv. 2 & 4 J. Stein,
v. 3 T. Smail

120

You shall go out with joy and be led forth with peace,
and the mountains and the hills shall break forth before you.
There'll be shouts of joy and the trees of the field
shall clap, shall clap their hands,
and the trees of the field shall clap their hands,
and the trees of the field shall clap their hands,
and the trees of the field shall clap their hands
and you'll go out with joy.

S. Dauermann

ACKNOWLEDGEMENTS

The Panel on Worship of the Church of Scotland and Oxford University Press thank the following who have given permission for copyright material to be included. Every effort has been made to trace copyright owners, and the compilers apologize to anyone whose rights have inadvertently not been acknowledged. An asterisk denotes a translation. Particulars of copyright music will be found in the full music edition.

Author	Hymn number	Text used by permission of
Adkins, D.	27	Word UK
Appleford, P.	72, 84	Josef Weinberger Ltd.
Bell, J.	11, 16, 21, 23, 36, 51, 54, 101, 112, 118	Wild Goose Publications (Iona Community)
Bilbrough, D.	3	Thankyou Music
Briggs, A.	113	Wild Goose Publications (Iona Community)
Carter, S.	47, 90	Stainer & Bell Ltd.
Chisholm, T. O.	37	Hope Publishing Company
Coelho, T.	26	Word UK
Colvin, T.	1, 46*, 60, 63, 80*	Hope Publishing Company
Cowie, I.	66	Wild Goose Publications (Iona Community)
Cullen, T.	8	Celebration (Thankyou Music)
Cunningham, I. D.	35	Author
Dale, A.	34	Oxford University Press
Dauermann, S.	120	Lillenas Publishing Company
Dunn, F.	59*	Thankyou Music
Dyer, M.	50	Celebration (Thankyou Music)
Farjeon, E.	78	David Higham Associates
Fishel, D.	7	Word of God Music
Fraser, I.	70	Stainer & Bell Ltd.
Frostenson, A.	77	Author
Galloway, K.	30, 87	Wild Goose Publications (Iona Community)
Gillman, B.	13	Thankyou Music
Green F. Pratt	82, 116	Stainer & Bell Ltd.
Hadden, D. J.	68	Restoration Music Ltd.
Hayford, J. W.	75	Rocksmith Music (admin. by Leosong Copyright Service Ltd.)
Hine, S.	86*	Thankyou Music
Howard, P. Thl	88	American Catholic Press
Icarus, P.	103	McCrimmon Publishing Co. Ltd.
Iona Community	12, 25, 74	Wild Goose Publications (Iona Community)
Iverson, D.	98	Moody Bible Institute of Chicago
Kaan, F.	29, 41, 65, 96	Stainer & Bell Ltd.
Kendrick, G.	56	Thankyou Music
Lafferty, K.	93	Word UK
Lewis, D.	77*	Author (translator)
Lundy, D.	102	Kevin Mayhew Ltd.
Lythgoe, L.	53*	Author (translator)
McCann, C.	32	Kevin Mayhew Ltd.
McClellan, S.	22	Thankyou Music
Maraschin, J.	53	Author
Markland, G.	24	Kevin Mayhew Ltd.
Maule, G.	11, 16, 21, 23, 36, 51, 54, 101, 112, 118	Wild Goose Publications (Iona Community)
Mills, P.	119	Fred Bock Music Co.
Monahan, D.	57*	Methodist Church Division of Education and Youth
Nyberg, A.	31, 39, 108	Wild Goose Publications (Iona Community)
	110	Wessmans Musikforlag, Sweden
Owens, C.	33	Word UK
Pac, J.	22	Thankyou Music
Perry, M.	81	Jubilate Hymns Ltd. (© M. Perry)
Quinn, J.	19	Geoffrey Chapman (a division of Cassell Publishers Ltd.)
Ryecroft, K.	22	Thankyou Music
Sands, E.	95	Magnificat Music (© E. Sands)
Scholtes, P.	111	FEL Publications
Scobie, A.	69, 73, 117	Panel on Worship of the Church of Scotland
Silvester, R.	68	Restoration Music Ltd.
Smail, T. A.	119 (v. 3)	Author
Smith, L. E. Jnr.	45	Thankyou Music
Stassen, L.	94	New Song Ministries
Stein, J.	119 (vv. 2 & 4)	Handsel Publications
Taizé Community	6, 15, 58, 79, 85, 99, 100, 109	© Les Presses de Taizé; published by Wm Collins Ltd.
Taylor, H.	63*	Hope Publishing Company
Temple, S.	76	Franciscan Communications Centre
White, E.	67	Kevin Mayhew Ltd.
	89	McCrimmon Publishing Co. Ltd.
White, I.	44, 64, 92	Little Misty Music
Wren, B.	10, 20, 28, 42, 71, 104	Oxford University Press

INDEX OF SONGS

Where titles differ from first lines they are shown in italic.